Rollercoaster of Emotions

Adonijah Niles

Dedication

I dedicate this book to my children. They have been the reasons why I push myself hard each day. They are the heartbeats to my lifeline.

Table of Contents

Love

A four-letter word
yet it holds so much weight.
I can't remember when
I first fell in love, but
I'm sure it was in 1994
when I first had contact with
the one who birthed me.
Yeah, the one who carried me
for 9 months.
We call her Ma now.
Or, maybe it was that man that
was beside the hospital bed?
I call him dad, but he's not here now.
I guess love was a feeling,
whether I felt it or not at that moment,
I can tell it felt me.
For some reason I would like to think
maybe I was love in human form.
Sounds crazy, I know. But,
do we truly know what love means?
Or, is our interpretation a figment of
own imagination or assumption of what it should be

Grief

The very feeling, we dread most.
For me, it occurred in the year 2003.
On the fifteenth of November, I saw the T.V.
Ma was downstairs with a look on her face
Displaced emotions, face frozen
Just to hear the man she loved is dead.
I'm heartbroken.
Grief,
You want to talk about a pain
that won't subside,
that's the kind of pain
that didn't feel good until I cried.
Tears now dried,
I have no choice but to smile,
Even though I myself felt dead inside.
How could you not grieve?
My father is gone
Who's gonna come teach me?
Who's gonna tell me about
the birds and the bees,
the real from the fake,
and the gents from the sleaze?

Depression

Who would have thought me?
The vibrant ever-growing tree,
would ever feel depressed?
The bright-eyed young lady
would lay a soul to rest?
Yes, a mother too young
conceived and birthed a son,
only to find no air in his lungs.
Suffocated.
I anticipated a life,
selfless to give to a child
that I still was myself.
Being grown only caused
me a swollen stomach.
I was smart, but being smart
didn't matter when my
displaced emotions told on itself.
Once again brokenhearted.
Seems like that became the norm.

Guilt

I believe I was twelve.
Sitting in a house
I was more than familiar with.
But who would've thought
that it wasn't safe?
A place
I couldn't go back to.
A place
I don't want to remember
because in that place
I was violated.
Laying on the couch sleeping
after all the drama that arose.
I felt your presence,
but I couldn't move.
I was stuck in a place of not knowing.
What was going to happen next, but
then it happened.
heard your footsteps
As you walked away.
I heard the door creak as you closed it.
Who do I tell?
Who will believe?
Guilt
Was it my fault?
Was it something I wore?
Was it because I was developed
in ways that can be sexualized by the human eye?
Do I keep this to myself, or do I tell?
I just want to yell,
"WHY ME?"

Aggression

So much built-in anger
needs an outlet to release.
Slick comments and stares
didn't fly with me.
Yet no one really knew the secrets
that laid deep in my heart.
No one understood my pain.
Aggression
Yelling at my teachers and fellow classmates,
using foul language and smoking weed,
I acted out.
I was justified!
You didn't walk in my shoes.
Aggression
MAD MAD MAD
Fights were normal.
Suspensions were normal.
My mind strictly carnal.
No one could tell me anything
Their words didn't mean a thing
because they didn't know how full
my heart was of hurt and betrayal.
They didn't know the burden I carried.
Was this my life,
or that of a movie?
Where's Jim Carey?
I need to laugh because
this aggression is haunting me.

Loneliness

I guess I was doing too much.
The mental Institute became my new home.
Doctors giving medicine
to try to calm me, not realizing
I just need someone to hear me.
Zoloft and Seroquel became my best friend.
Walking like a zombie
down the hall with all the other
young men and women.
Fourteen years old dealing with mental depression.
Loneliness
No one to turn to,
No one to count on.
Left alone for everyone else to deal with.
Leaving the institute
To live with more people who didn't want me.
I was damaged goods.
So much to offer, yet such a liability.
They wouldn't say it, but I could see it.
Crazy how they could
disown you so naturally.
I had to make moves that
I would later in life regret.

Hope

At sixteen I became a mother.
Pregnant again yet so young.
I was determined to be a better mother
than the example I had.
I was determined to give
my baby the life I didn't.
She deserved it.
Little kicks to forehead kisses,
she gave me peace.
My Eunyece.
Her name stands for victory,
which is what I received
when having her.
God was on my side.
I was down for the ride.
Went to church and got saved,
baptized in the Holy Ghost
and speaking in tongues.
I grew in the faith
and God spoke to me even more.
I was excited because for once in all my life
I was happy.
This all felt right.
Hope
Is what I got when I trusted in God,
but I didn't always stay there.
I fell astray multiple times, but
Hope brought me back

Forgiveness

I had to learn that.
Not only to forgive others,
but how to forgive myself.
More times too often
no matter what was done,
I would forgive the other person,
but I never released myself from it;
as if I was punishing myself for what happened.
It took a deep encounter with God,
an "I am Lord and you are my child" moment.
I found myself growing.
I found myself sowing
Into good ground.
I found myself forgiving myself.
Forgiveness
I found chains broken,
Generational curses ceased,
Bondages torn.
I found myself clean and redeemed.
I found myself a Child of God.
I found myself as a King's Kid,
I found myself how God seen me.
I found myself a sheep to the Shepard.
I found myself having visions and dreams.
I found myself talking to God.
I found myself ministering.
I found myself winding back into my old ways.
No one said that this path was easy

Part Two Coming Summer 2021:

Rollercoaster of Emotions Pt. 2

About the Author

About the Author

Born in the Bronx, N.Y, but raised in Albany, *Adonijah Niles* has seen and had many trials that motivated her to want to become an author. *Adonijah* has faced many things from sexual and physical abuse, rejection, teen pregnancy, and prison just to name a few. Yet, her story doesn't end there. With all that she went through, *Adonijah* wants to be a voice for many young women and mothers to guide them and show them that their story isn't over yet and there is greater to come. *Adonijah* has attended the Midwest College of Theology receiving her Bachelor of Arts Degree in Biblical Studies.

Adonijah loves to sing and has written a host of songs, one including 'Hem of your Garment.' Adonijah has three children whom she loves dearly. To learn more about Adonijah Niles, you can follow her on her Facebook, Clubhouse, and Instagram.

Facebook: www.facebook.com/addieprayse

Clubhouse: @addieprayse

Instagram: @addieprayse

Acknowledgements

Acknowledgements

I want to take this time to acknowledge some of those that has been a part of my journey and has either helped or been my support throughout. First and foremost, I want to thank God for all I went through because I wouldn't be the woman I am today. Each situation helped me to become better and stronger every day. For that I am grateful and forever thankful. Secondly my children, whom I conceived through my struggle. They not only went through with me, but they saw our overcoming and how God made a way out of no way. Thirdly, my best friend Na'Kenya Bonner aka Mrs. Davidson. She has held me up for the longest at times when the ones I thought needed to be there were not. She took me in as her sister and her family accepted me as such. With that, I say thank you all. You have all inspired me in more ways than you know.

I love you all

www.ingramcontent.com/pod-product-compliance
Lightning Source LLC
Chambersburg PA
CBHW072012280526
45788CB00005B/2012